Dear Self

Move With The Wind

Read When...

This book is dedicated to the high school and college students. As a college student myself, I find it difficult to "move with the wind," considering that the young adult stage is the time where we begin to discover ourselves.

You Need to Move With The Wind (Encouragement)

Dear Self,

Today, I will move with the wind. In order to do that, I will do the following:

a.)

b.)

c.)

Love,
 Yourself

Dear Self,

Stand up from the ground. I know that it's hard to be motivated right now, but just know that whatever it is that you are pursuing is for your loved ones and for your community. So, utilize your gifts and talents to move with the wind. Otherwise, the community may end up suffering the loss of a wonderful person.

Love,
Yourself

Dear Self,

You are not meant to remain on the floor.

Yes, you had a challenge and yes you encountered something that you did not choose to encounter, but guess what, things happen for a reason. Every incident teaches you a lesson. What type? Take from the lesson and reflect on it. Don't hinder yourself from growing, everyone makes mistakes. Now get up and move with the wind.

Love,
Yourself

Dear Self,

You have the right to feel. Don't apologize for any emotions that you're having. If you're sad, you're sad. If you're mad, you're mad. Don't apologize for having feelings. You are perfectly fine. It's okay to come to school tired, it's okay to wake up and not feel like you want to wear makeup. You are perfect, and don't feel bad for feeling a certain way.

Love,
 Yourself

Dear Self,

You have the right to feel, you have the right to protect yourself. It's always nice to be nice, but when people push you over your edge, say something. There's a difference between getting pushed over and pushing your emotions. There's a balance. You know your self worth, don't let people treat you like crap.

Love,
 Yourself

Dear Self,

People will try to discourage you, they will try to dissuade you from following the wind.
But you know what, just keep moving. Just keep on pursuing your dreams. don't ever abandon your goal or your plans just because someone says that you can't. When people say this, it is because of their ability not to surpass anything. Don't get stomped on, keep moving with the wind.

Love,
Yourself

Dear Self,

Don't ever be afraid to move different paths of the winds. Surpassing your boundaries is hard, but you can never truly know what you're capable of unless you've exceeded your boundaries.

Love,
 Yourself

Dear Self,

Stop saying that you can't do things because of a
certain aspect. Make the most of your given resources
and work from there. You don't necessarily need
everything to work and start from scratch. Whatever
you do, always keep moving with the wind.

Love,
 Yourself

Dear Self,

Trust yourself— no one knows how hard you work, the sacrifices you have made, the amount of frustrations you have encountered, and the boundaries that you surpassed. It's okay to seek for guidance, but you have to rely on yourself, NOT the approval of others. You learn the value of hard work by working hard. So, move with your wind and at your own pace.

Love,
  Yourself

Dear Self,

It's okay to make mistakes, it's okay to sway against the wind, You're growing and finding new currents. What's not okay is that you stay stuck in that current. Move, push yourself to be the best version of yourself. These are the mistakes that I learned from today, and this is what I will do to fix it:

a.)

b.)

c.)

Love,
 Yourself

You Are Unsure of Which Wind to Sway With

(Trouble with loved ones)

Dear Self,

You carry a special seed that is made to be branched out into a tree. Surround yourself with a flock of birds who will carry your seed, and move you into a safe location, those who will make sure that your seed is safe and will enable you to branch out into the tree that you are destined to be.

Love,
 Yourself

Dear Self,

Don't stoop to their level. People will talk behind your back, and not everyone will like you, but as long as you know your worth, you know what your capabilities are, then that's what matters.

Love,
 Yourself

Dear Self,

People will try to bring you down. they will try to compare their capacity level to yours, but you know what, push that aside because YOU determine your capacity level, you decide what boundaries you want to surpass. Whatever you are able to do, you can achieve.

Love,
 Yourself

Dear Self,

I know that you're surrounded by a bunch of different coworkers or classmates who have values that don't even resonate with you, but the truth is, not everyone's the same. We are all on one planet for a reason, we are designed to think differently, and we contribute a gift that is different from the rest. Don't latch onto those who are not like you, move with the wind and find those that you have commonalities with. Don't be afraid!

Love,
 Yourself

Dear Self,

A true queen is someone who constantly uplifts the souls around her and someone who empowers other women by supporting and guiding them.

Love,
 Yourself

Dear Self,

Don't move with the wind by yourself when achieving a goal, find the same feathers that flock together with you, find those that you can hover the clouds with, those who can share the same worm as you, and those who are willing to land with you.

Love,
 Yourself

Dear Self,

I know that it's hard to be surrounded by those who don't believe in you. It's hard to be the best version of yourself when you're surrounded with those who just constantly belittle you and put you down. But guess what, you are more than what they say about you. Sometimes, the reason why they say negative things about you is because it is a reflection of themselves. They're probably frustrated with their reflection. Just know your worth, know that you carry value, know that you contribute something in this society. You have a gift that stands apart from everyone else. Believe in yourself.

Love,
 Yourself

Dear Self,

When you don't find someone cheering along the way for you, don't be discouraged. You are your own cheerleader. You can do this.

Love,
 Yourself

Dear Self,

I know that you are irritated with some of your family members, but know that this is your life. You are in control of your happiness. If you are feeling a certain way, let them know because no one can detect your emotions.

Love,
 Yourself

When you Need to Embrace Your Route of Wind (Self love)

Dear Self,

I love you, and these are the reasons why:

a.)

b.)

c.)

Love,
  Yourself

Dear Self,

You are trying your best. You don't have to follow a specific formula in order to structure yourself to function with the world. You move with the wind at your own pace, don't be tied up in a hurricane or a puff of air. You set your current and you set your speed.

Love,
 Yourself

Dear Self,

I know that you were moving through a hurricane yesterday, but today is a brand new day. Take all of the things that you learned and create something new with it. You are better than yesterday. You can do this.

Love,
 Yourself

Dear Self,

Smile. Although today was a day filled with challenges, you overcame them! Don't forget to note that these challenges piece up the puzzle to your future. You got stronger.

Love,
Yourself

Dear Self,

You fell, and that's okay. What's not okay is sitting still. Get up, stand up, and keep walking. You never know what you'll achieve if you're there sitting in the floor, pondering your mistakes.

Love,
Yourself

Dear Self,

You possess such strong talents and gifts that differ from other people. STOP comparing yourself to others. If you continue to look side to side, then you will never unravel those gifts. The community can actually lose someone with such talent, so stop looking around and look straight ahead, 'cause, darlin', you are amazing.

Just to remind myself, these are my gifts:
a.)

b.)

c.)

Love,
Yourself

Dear Self,

Stand up, look at your challenges straight in the face, and say, "Hey, I've got this." Each and every day, we are faced with obstacles, not as a way to inhibit us from achieving our goals, but as a way to learn from them. Didn't achieve your 50 pushups in the gym.. Okay, why? Didn't get a promotion… okay, why? These hurdles are a way for us to learn from our mistakes, to reassess our methods, and to ultimately become better versions of ourselves. So wake up Beauty, it's time to beast.

Love,
 Yourself

Dear Self,

Don't be afraid to be you! You are a gem, and don't you ever forget that!

Love,
 Yourself

Dear Self,

You do not need anyone to complete you, you complete
yourself. You don't need
Anyone to walk home with you nor fight those battles
with you. You are strong, that's why you're here in
this world, you are strong enough to live it. You can do
this. Get up, look your fear straight in the eye, and
conquer it. Because beauty, it's definitely time to
beast.

Love,
 Yourself

Dear Self,

What is the big picture? Sometimes when we fail in life or have results that may not be as expected, we discourage ourselves. We want results fast, and if they don't work out, we tend to give up and lose faith. Just know that whatever obstacles you're encountering in your life, you are able to triumph them. You can achieve anything that you desire as long as you have the passion to dream it, the courage to plan it, and the faith to attain it.

Love,
 Yourself

Dear Self,

Love yourself. We live in an environment where we are dictated to by society; if an individual deviates from a certain norm, then we are looked down upon to the point where we question our own identity. So regardless of where everything stands, embrace who you are and be humble towards yourself, because in the end, we'll all be judged one way or another. So continue loving your quirks and your strengths. After all, life would be pretty dreary if we were the same, right?

Love,
Yourself

Dear Self,

Dance in the rain, scream your lungs out, cry when you want to cry, and smile every chance that you get (okay, probably not every time.) Whatever it is, live your life and be in paradise, center your soul in the universe, and everything will fall into place

Love,
 Yourself

Dear Self,

You are a true royal. A person with this title is someone who constantly uplifts the souls around her and someone who empowers others by supporting and guiding them. COntinue to do that for those in our community. Because, Darling, how will you make people move with the wind with you?

Love,
 Yourself

Dear Self,

I can't help but think about the past, about how motivated and strong suited you were. Guess what, you still are! Things are constantly evolving, we are put in a position for a reason. Maybe it's to strengthen your emotional being, maybe it's to one day help someone who needs it, maybe it's just to take you out of your comfort zone, and make you realize that you are more than just a letter grade or more than just a numerical number on a scale. So stop putting yourself down.

Love,
 Yourself

Dear Self,

I know that there are times where you gear towards the past because you were happy the way things were, but the truth is, life is evolving. Change is constant, you can't expect them to be steady. You find new methods, find new friends, and find new things that work for you. You discover yourself, discover your purpose, and discover your being. You can't do that by being stuck in your boundaries. Surpass those boundaries, and grow with the seed. Blossom like the tree that you are meant to be, and sway with the winds.

Love,
 Yourself

Dear Self,

Sometimes it's okay to be lost-- you can find rocks surrounded with sand, you can find leaves surrounded with branches, and you can find a pair of pink shoes surrounded with blue ones. It's okay to lose yourself, because when you lose yourself, you move with the wind to see where you belong.

Love,
 Yourself

Dear Self,

Sometimes we become people that we never thought that we would be: the person that pushes others away, the person who wants be isolated from the world, the person who eats French fries, even though you vow not to, but you know what, that's okay. We're always in a different place where we want to discover ourselves, to discover our purpose, and to discover where we fit in with the world. So don't apologize. If you want to stay steady as a rock, then hey, why not? But, always remember that the rock always moves, especially in times where the wind blows heavily.

Love,
 Yourself

Dear Self,

I love you. I vow to always move with the wind.

Love,
  Yourself

About the Author

Lyka Camille Raza is currently a college senior at Chaminade University of Honolulu. She is currently double majoring in biology and english and minoring in psychology. She aspires to one day become a physician. She realizes that reading letters to oneself will uplift one's spirit. The goal of this book is to make a positive contribution to those in her community. She ultimately believes that writing a letter to others in the community will inspire others to push their best self.